# And Peace on Earth

## Bob Chilcott

*A Christmas cantata for female vocalist (or solo alto), children's choir, SATB choir, piano, bass, brass ensemble, and two percussion players*

Vocal score

MUSIC DEPARTMENT

**OXFORD**
UNIVERSITY PRESS

# OXFORD
### UNIVERSITY PRESS

Great Clarendon Street, Oxford OX2 6DP, England
198 Madison Avenue, New York, NY10016, USA

Oxford University Press is a department of the University of Oxford.
It furthers the University's aim of excellence in research, scholarship,
and education by publishing worldwide in

Oxford New York
Auckland Cape Town Hong Kong Karachi
Kuala Lumpur Madrid Melbourne Mexico City Nairobi
New Delhi Shanghai Taipei Toronto

With offices in

Argentina Austria Brazil Chile Czech Republic France Greece
Guatemala Hungary Italy Japan Poland Portugal Singapore
South Korea Switzerland Thailand Turkey Ukraine Vietnam

Oxford is a registered trade mark of Oxford University Press
in the UK and in certain other countries

10

ISBN 978-0-19-335566-8

Music and text origination by Jeanne Roberts
Printed in Great Britain on acid-free paper by
Halstan & Co. Ltd., Amersham, Bucks.

# Contents

# Composer's note

I have designed this piece to embrace a variety of styles, hence the female vocalist (or solo alto) should ideally be comfortable singing in a jazz style. The vocalist should be amplified, along with the bass (which can be string or electric), and possibly the piano too, depending on the acoustics of the performance space.

Duration: *c.*17 minutes

*And Peace on Earth* is scored for piano, electric or string bass, five trumpets (one doubling on flugelhorn), two trombones, one bass trombone, tuba, and two percussion players. The full score and parts are available to hire from the publisher.

*Commissioned by the City of Birmingham Choir for its Christmas Celebration in Symphony Hall, Birmingham, on 19 December 2004, with support from the Birmingham Common Good Trust, the Dumbreck Charity, the John Feeney Charitable Trust, and the Edward and Dorothy Cadbury Trust*

# And Peace on Earth

## 1. *The time draws near*

Alfred, Lord Tennyson (1809–92)

BOB CHILCOTT

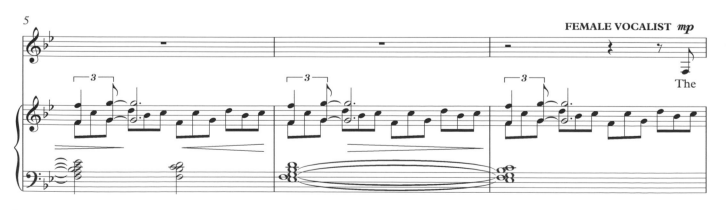

*Alternatively, this part may be sung by a solo alto.

**8**

time draws near the birth of Christ: the moon is hid; the night is still; The

**10**

Christ-mas bells from hill to hill__ An-swer each o - ther in the mist.__ Four

**12** **FEMALE VOCALIST**

voi-ces of__ four ham-lets round, From far and near, on mead and moor; Swell out and fail, as if a door Were

S.

Peace and good-will, good-will and peace, peace and good-will__ to

A.

Peace and good-will, good-will and peace, peace and good-will__ to

T.

Peace and good-will, good-will and peace, peace and good-will__ to

B.

Peace__ and good - will, good - will and peace, peace and good-will__ to

year I slept and woke with pain, I al-most wished no more to wake, And that my hold on life would break be-

-fore I heard those bells a - gain, those bells a - gain.

But they my trou-bled spi-rit rule, For

They bring me sor-row touched with joy, The

they con-trolled me when a boy;

*attacca*

# 2. Good day, Sir Christemas

Anon., mid 15th-cent. English

**Lively and rhythmic** ♩ = *c*.144

¹snelle = are aware

<sup>2</sup> clerkys = writer    <sup>3</sup> balys = sorrows

All man-ner of mirths we wole make

And so-lace to our hearts take, My

seme-ly lord, for your sake. Good

day, good day, good day.

*attacca*

# 3. *This endris night*

Anon., 15th-cent. English

[1] endris = other

hay?

hay?

My sweet-est bird thus 'tis re - quired, Though thou be king ve -

**FEMALE VOCALIST**

- ray; But ne-ver-the-less__ I will not cease To sing, by, by, lul -

**FEMALE VOCALIST**

-lay.'

S.
A.

The child then spake in his talk - ing, And

T.
B.

cresc.

209 **FEMALE VOCALIST**

all thy_ will I would ful - fil Thou know - est well, in_ fay;² And for all this_ I

S.
A.

All thy will I would ful - fil,_____ And will thee___

T.
B.

thee

214

will thee kiss,_ And sing, by, by, lul - lay.'_____

kiss, And sing, by, by, lul - lay.'_____

219 *mp espress.*

Oh, my son,_ my sweet son.

My dear mo - ther, when time it be,_____ Take thou me up

My dear mo - ther, when time it be, time it be,

My dear mo - ther, when time it be, it be, me up

² fay = faith

247 A tempo                               FEMALE VOCALIST *mp*

'Now sweet son, since

*mp*

252 it is come so, That all is at thy will, I pray thee grant to me_ a_ boon,

257 If it be right and skill³

262 FEMALE VOCALIST *mf*

That child or_ man, who will_ or_ can Be mer-ry on my day,

*cresc.*

S. who can Be mer-ry on my day, To

*mf*

A. who can Be mer-ry on my day, To

*mf* *cresc.*

T. That child or man, Be mer-ry on my day, To

*mf*

B. That child or man, Be mer-ry on my day,_____ To

*mf*

³skill = reasonable

# 4. *Put memory away*

Elizabeth Jennings (1926–2001)

This movement is also available as a separate leaflet (ISBN 978–0–19–343337–3).

Text by Elizabeth Jennings; by permission of David Higham Associates.
Music © Oxford University Press 2005 and 2006.

24

attacca

# 5. *Run, shepherds, run*

William Drummond of Hawthornden (1585–1649)

*If performing this movement as a separate piece without the bass, brass, and percussion accompaniment, the pianist is encouraged to *ad lib.* on the reduction.

- row\_\_ swad - dlings are our spheres.

Run, shep - herds, run,\_\_ run, run.

run, run, run, run, run.

**FEMALE VOCALIST**

This is that night

no, day that day grown great with bliss,\_